Frances Corkey Thompson

Wild Gooseberries
of Hailung

Indigo Dreams Publishing

First Edition: Wild Gooseberries of Hailung
First published in Great Britain in 2015 by:
Indigo Dreams Publishing
24, Forest Houses
Cookworthy Moor
Halwill
Beaworthy
Devon
EX21 5UU

www.indigodreams.co.uk

ISBN 978-1-909357-67-9

British Library Cataloguing in Publication Data. A CIP record for this book can be obtained from the British Library.

Designed and typeset in Palatino Linotype by Indigo Dreams.
Cover design by Ronnie Goodyer at Indigo Dreams
Cover image by Frances Corkey Thompson
Printed and bound in Great Britain by 4edge Ltd
www.4edge.co.uk
Papers used by Indigo Dreams are recyclable products made from wood grown in sustainable forests following the guidance of the Forest Stewardship Council.

for my mother Doreen,
remembering Dad

Acknowledgements

I wish to thank my Mandarin teacher Wu Chia-Chen, my guides and translators in China, Song Lele and Dan Zhang, and my good friend and travelling-companion Chris Williams. My gratitude goes also to Helena Nelson of HappenStance Press and to the poet Ruth O'Callaghan for the generosity of their time and wisdom, and to the editors of the magazines and anthologies where some of the poems in this collection first had an outing.

The poem "Traveller Talk" will appear in Poetry Ireland Review, no 114, 2015.

"Goddess of Mercy" was a prizewinner in the 2014 Manchester Cathedral Competition. It was read in the Cathedral and published in its booklet.

"The Changes" appeared in The Frogmore Papers, no 84, 2014.

"Pouring Tea" appeared in Wherever, Cinnamon Press, 2006.

A version of "By Lough Neagh" appeared in Irish Pages, 2003.

Versions of other poems were published in Four in The Morning, an anthology from Soaring Penguin Press, 2012.

CONTENTS

Wild Gooseberries
of Hailung

Foreword

When I was four, a Chinese friend of Dad's came to stay with us in Castlederg, Co. Tyrone. We called him Mr Li. His full name was *Li T'ing Ku'ei*. We missed him when he left. I learned when I grew up, that after his return to China, Mr Li suffered a dreadful fate. I am glad to remember him in this book.

Dad had been a missionary in China before I was born. In the decades leading up to WW2, ninety-one missionaries from the Irish Presbyterian Church went to the north-eastern part of China known as Manchuria. My father was one of them, dedicating his life to Manchuria. However, his first five years, 1936 -1941, were to be his only time there. Missionaries were forced by the Japanese to leave, and the ban was later reinforced by Mao Tse Tung. For the rest of his working life, my father was a Presbyterian minister in Ireland.

In our home, an ivory *Gwan Yin* presided on the mantelpiece. A fat Buddha squatted on the hall table. Books on Chinese history and philosophy filled the shelves of my father's study, Confucius and Lao Tse keeping company with Kierkegaard and Bonhoeffer. There were also the albums for poring over, packed with small black-and-white photos showing my young father in his other place, his other time.

Shortly after my early retirement from teaching, I was telling my mother about a friend who had typed out old family documents for posterity. "You could do that with your father's letters," she said. "What letters?" I asked. "Letters he wrote from China," she said, "to your grandparents." It was the first I'd heard of them.

Working with Dad, now in his eighties, I edited the letters into a book, which eventually took on a life of its own. Dad's letters are read in many countries, and formed the basis of a BBC documentary series.

All the letters, to and from Manchuria, had travelled by train through Siberia.

Shortly after Dad died, I decided to go to Manchuria, now called Dongbei. Photos of 1930s China scanned well. Mr Li stepped forward out of my memory of him. I prepared booklets of Dad's photos and writings. These would be my passports, justification for turning up in places so very far removed from the tourist trail.

For my first visit in 2009, I contacted Chris Williams. We had travelled together before, and she understood my ways. I wrote, "I'm going to China, want to come?" She e-mailed back "Yes." "Via Siberia, the railway", I said. "OK," she replied. We flew to Moscow and boarded the train. The two-week trans-Siberian journey, a wonder in its own right, allowed time and space for reflection.

In Dongbei, Chris took notes and kept me organised. For the people we met, their history started in 1959 – few records have survived. Buildings and books were destroyed. People, too, were destroyed in millions. Of some of Dad's places, we found neither trace nor record. In other towns and villages, vast new churches towered over wreckage.

It was in these places that I handed the booklets over. Old people touched my face, stared at each other, bent over the photos pointing and exclaiming at the young fellow with white-blond hair laughing with Chinese friends. "He was called *Gao K'e Li,*" I told them. "He lived here. Do you remember him?"

Tonghua, Manchuria, 1939

The author with Mr Li and her parents, Ireland, 1949

The Changes

Now that he's gone
the books crowding his study –
the histories, the theologies, the Lao Tse – all
are beginning to lose sight of him

and in the old Manchuria photos
he's a grown child, a brother,
somebody's grandson, my young
remembered father.

Language School

Jabbing at his own chest, the teacher was making
the noise of a newborn calf. *Wǒ!* First person singular.
To the Derry man falling in love with China,
words and their lilt came easy

as they would later to his child.
I could warble a Mandarin *Jesus Loves Me* before I knew
this language was hard. Those were the days
of the spell and the pull of China.

On a Donegal strand my spade tore
a Mandarin *man* up out of the sand's skin
and another one, and more.
By teatime the sea had flattened them.

The fourth tone works if you duck your chin.
You can practise all of them in the rhyme
about mother riding the slow horse and cursing –
mā mā qí mǎ, mǎ màn, mā mā mà mǎ.

Cliff-Fall

She knows the place backwards – Donegal
through long refracted twilights. Her tin spade scrapes
man into the sand, two-legged, Mandarin.
There is no cloud. She does not see

the cliff or the two birds whirring
like puppets powered by a crazy hand.
Make another Chinese man.
Angle the blade so the drawn furrows of sand

topple over themselves like ploughing.
Expert, she makes an army.
Stay with me, he said in a dream that saw out the day.
Stay with me. She will stay. The road

cuts up and round and away but land
slips, eclipses. How it lies.

The Broad Road

Where does it end? I'd ask over the wall
of adult shoulders, road filling the windscreen.
Not McMullan's Lane with its grassy stripe
along the middle, not the daisy-trail
across the field to school, but what we called
the Broad Road. *Tell me, where does it end, the road?*
Round the next corner? No, there's more, far more.
Over the world a maze of ways, a mist
you're lost in. Follow the breadcrumb path and find
that weathers, at least, are faithfully various –
needles of frost creeping over Siberia,
news of an early snowfall in Manchuria.

Scanning Mr Li

My screen is grey but I remember the brown
of Mr Li's good face, his hand at my shoulder, my blue
jersey with elephants, my eczema's blaze,

how he bewitched us all the day he took
the manse kitchen over from Mum and cooked a banquet.
Ballooned in steam and banging random pans, he surfaced

with dishes of slippery *jiaodze*.
After he left us it was years before they told me
he had died. And how. And why.

Did your new creed flex muscle like a minder, Mr Li?
Or did you cry in your agony to the Goddess of Mercy and yearn
for simple days of Moonfeasts?

The rest of us grew into ourselves, suffered
nothing. An old photo is shot through with new light
but for Li T'ing Ku'ei in the quiet Ulster whin

nothing stirs.

She Scribbles on Green

post-it notes, a host of them.
They sprout from her book like grass.

He would pause in his reading, reach
for notebook and fountain pen to record

precisely, noting the page, adding some notions
to consider that might lead

closer but they lead, as always,
away, and there is no notebook, no eloquent ink,

only something given and withheld –
the pencil blunt, grass growing.

Separation

A light burns
and is not consumed.

Lives have touched
that will not touch again.

Between here and there –
ten thousand miles
and a few billion people.

Degrees of separation –
one.

The Mei-Ling Book

Here – is – Mei-Ling. She – is – a – Chinese – girl.
Look – at – her – coat – and – trousers.
"Good – morning," she – says.

I explain to my mother and father
that if I had been born in China instead of Belfast
I would look just like Mei-Ling.

No, they say, *you would look like you.*
A tunic and pyjama trousers will show them –
Here I am. A Chinese Girl.

Still they do not understand.

Having Invented

astronomy, horology, metallurgy,
theory of music, reed instruments, the five-note scale,
the seismograph,
paper, printing, movable type,
paper money, decimalisation,
the abacus, the magnetic compass,
gunpowder, land mines, fireworks,
engineering, navigation,
water wheels, paddle wheels, agriculture –
irrigation, seed drill, the plough,
domestication of ox and buffalo,

noodles,
kites,
silk,

and having discovered
fossils, blood circulation
and the causes of solar and lunar eclipses,

having been, for millennia,
a civilisation,

why would you want

Presbyterians?

Suitcase

It isn't the leaving home
nor it is the anticipation
nor that the time has finally arrived,
it's the suitcase.

After the panics, the packing,
the unpacking and re-packing
of clothes, footwear, food,
the googling and the forecasts,

photos and documents,
his visiting card, his name in Hanyu,
in Pinyin, in Putonghua,
in my head –

the snap of its lock.
Its neat wheels and good black bulges.
The tight
bright green strap.

Train

An English one is a drawing-room
where trees pirouette for you and the hills
click past each other like a clever Victorian toy –
disciplined, drawing attention.

On this train
we have parcelled out our days in raisins and biscuits,
counted soup-packets for the samovar
and the Earl Grey will last – just.

On this train
you can sleep through the Urals, Siberia doesn't care –
it needs no declarations
about its eternal hay-coloured distances

and this train provides absence
of interference. Engine business is down to a whisht.
Self is light,
unbodied as a letter.

Salt

A grown daughter is like smuggled salt – Chinese proverb

I am freight. I'm rolling stock without a logo
and not useful like salt. Having pirated his writings,
uncovered the key to his codes, I'm a late

delivery in a trade long halted, for this train
was the postal route, his time-shift link with home,
the long rein.

A dream of birthing –
of pushing the old man through to the light.
What did he withhold? All his letters home

censored and self-censored.
Aeneas wept in Troy:
Sunt lacrimae rerum et mentem mortalia tangunt.

At my borders I'll declare:
one set of memories, second-hand;
one baggage of genes stamped with his features.

The Sleeping Land

1

The Tartars called it *Sebiyr*.
Wraiths fly at your face in the moonlight.
Pull the blind, nest in the whoosh and thrum.
Lose ground. You are being shipped
backwards to Moscow, to Atlantic,
flimsy, diving the void like a feather, now snatched
by a woman in booted black who bolts through thickets
cramming you headfirst down into her long bag,
jolting old dreams out of their hidey-holes.

ll

Mornings. Stuck in the geography of your own body
you're shaken down like rice, grounded in your skin, parked.
A billion birches become *birch* becomes balance.

Smoke lifts from black dwellings out there on black soil.
Are root vegetables on the boil? Is the satellite dish rattled
by the wind whipping the grasses?

A woman is bending to her chickens.
A man walks in a brown field, casting no shadow.
Notions of home in the remotest of strangers.

After Krasnoyarsk

Time is no longer tyrant, but sits alongside us,
stating itself, if at all, in stations. The train clock
is stuck on Moscow time, at growing odds with the sun.

My brother is following me on Google Earth
but where I am is here, and relentlessly here. After Krasnoyarsk
grass has gone to seed, gone to hay, seen

and gone and seen. Gone. Heave at the door
of the fearsome hatch rancid with metal-spark and smoke
and smokers lurking. Heave at the next

to brave the chill and perilous moving-ground. Balance
in the undone hurtle and swing and let Siberia
hammer itself home to your skeleton's core.

Music

Tonight I knew the white room again, the white bed,
the unfathomable curtain,
the old song that swelled like a door opening,
both of us knowing his completion,
both lifted into the song.

Russia grumbles past in the night.
The music I hear is the strain that played for the old Letters –
Granny's news carried out east like me,
folded with the scrawl of the grandfather I never knew –
love and pride on these very rails.
And westward for five years, the letters of my father's days
heading home to this very same percussion.

Grace

Once, in the days when the King's Hall had an ice rink,
we skated together.
He wore his skates as if it had been yesterday,
leaning into his direction, feet winding the one over the other
rasping up clouds of ice.
We circled away to the edges and back, in touch,
with grace.
That one time.

Skating in Peking, he said. *Hou Hai Lake.*
Man dear it was powerful!

Keeping Us in Stitches

I knew him in the arch of his back,
delivering consolation as he would
at some poor soul's bedside

but no. Over there, they said,
pointing to where a new shape
curled over its own debility.

Not until he straightened and smiled
did I know him.
So very unlike the last time

when he'd had us all in stitches
zooming his wheelie Zimmer over the shiny floor,
dressing-gown trailing.

The Unfinished Conversation

After one of his final strokes
he woke
to a nurse whose family ran a Chinese restaurant

so he spoke to her in Mandarin.
But she, being a Belfast girl, assumed
the mind was going.

Pouring Tea

This is how tea is poured.
This is how we offer and accept, do with our hands
what hands do.

A safe green belt is around his name, and around the fact
of needing no sugar-bowl today, although we are all gathered,
We cling to the edges of sofas.

Is this how grubs get gravity's shift
when they slip from earth into sky?
This is the day we learn how 'widow' is said.

A person arrives with forms to fill. Fingers close
on the pen she offers. The pen
spills itself into the right boxes.

Let her papers be folded with care
and with tenderness
placed in the brown envelope for her to take away.

This is how steam rises when tea is poured.
This is how the lip flinches
at the first sip.

Under the Twin Spires of St Peter's

our grey city church held its own
from Harland & Wolff, from Gallahers, Mackies Foundry –
the loyal Protestant men, their women.

It was not what he had planned for his life –

not the muscular rectitude of garnering the heathen,
not a gentle mind-opener with a mountain temple priest,
no brave singing the Lord's song in a strange land –

this was a mission to be hammered out with his own fist:
"Our Roman Catholic fellow-countrymen
worship the same God as we do."

Then Mac hits the organ, his feet
working the pedals like a dancer, bodies rustle, voices rise
to greet, like a good friend, the Old Hundredth –

All people that in earth do dwell...
Devilment and doubt are harboured, for now,
in dusty glass-stained sunlight.

Chinese Proverb

The bird sings
not because it has an answer
but because it has a song

Lake Baikal Museum

Once in the Lake there is no going back –
not for the seals,
noses turned up for a sniff of their lost Arctic,
not for the fish, forced to remodel or die.

This specimen is known as The Baikal Fish of No Colour.
See the transparent skin, the empty flesh.

We peer though glass
at white bones, a thread of black gut,
a dot where the brain might be that managed
fathoms, rise and fall.

Rivers

find their way but blindly.
Having made their own beds, they tend to lie in them
forging on out of unmapped beginnings,
drawn to their own annihilation
like the Nile slithering into the Med
or the mighty Angara's northward haul to the Arctic,

and to be a river is dreaming,
running in sleep like a dog beneath a table
and rivers, when they freeze,
make travelling 'so much easier', wrote the missionaries.
There it goes, the Word of God,
skating out to the far regions.

The Steppe

So this is how people live in tents with painted wood
that they undo and lift and shift in the new season
with stoves and chimneys and ropes and toothbrushes
and their horses and their children.

Playing the nomad,
we shoulder rucksacks and cameras and leave
the thin desert twigs to spring up behind us
and the wind to score footprints out of the sand

where we have been.
And where is it exactly that we have been?
A real nomad carries the Centre of the Earth Pole with her
so she's always there.

Mongolia to Gobi

telegraph poles and telegraph poles
        and wires and wires and wires
and rickety fences made of sticks
        and fences made of tyres
and empty, empty, empty land
        and smoke from unseen fires
and a railway line that snakes away
        through telegraph poles and wires

.

Bright Moon – *Bú kān huí shōu*

The poet Li Bai saw moonlight
fall across his floor like frost.
He raised his head to look at the bright moon.
Lowered his head and thought of home.

If changes are great enough to cause unbearable sadness
Bú kān huí shōu may be said.

Where

where are you and the mist still on the river
and where are you with sun at this low height
and where are you when it is night
and me out in the loose and cranky world?

Blink you are there, the bulk of you, your hair, blink
you are not. You are under the hill they say
and I am watching the window
like a stupid girl waiting for the postman.

The Dining Car Enters China

In the same way as those beeches stand up
when you've passed Rackenford on the link road,
a hill has appeared

and is still shimmying backwards on the horizon
long after steppe has unrolled into desert.
A thousand years ago, the moon

was drinking companion to the poet
and here it comes again. You wrote, Dad,
that it rose over Culnady

at the same time as it was setting on Manchuria.
I think it hung at your Liaoyang wall
like a lamp you'd brought from home.

By Lough Neagh

In a bedlam of birds and breezes
I found a flat stone by the Lough.

My hands went in, refracted,
paling, and my arms to the elbow.

The hospital windows flashed
but the Lough was blind, and gathered,

thick-flecked, on me,
building a causeway to the sky.

My hands were fins, working
as if a creature could outwit water,

as if a person might fly unhinged
around the earth.

Overheard

On the Chinese train from Ulaan Bataar,
where the line parts company from the Vladivostock route
and heads south-east
through engineered mountains and magnificent lakes
down towards Beijing
I heard the guard say to the other guard
a word I recognised to mean *What?* –

and then I heard sounds I understood as
eight, correct, certainly is, one,
a thousand, look, one minute,
haven't, haven't, should, China,
look, look, look again, and
OK, which means
OK.

Hooray!

At Hou Hai Lake, Beijing

Beyond the willow island
a brown sky blanks out the city.
The grand lily umbrellas of the Lake
have toppled back into themselves.

In Beijing I'm semi-literate.
In Manchuria, which is DongBei, I'll be as good as dumb.
What will they do with me? Was is sensible to bring
photos of grandchildren?

Water chestnuts, seaweed, trees' ears
arrive wrapped in a lily pad.
Yellow chrysanthemums bloom inside a glass teapot.
How come I'm suddenly so good with chopsticks?
Even the slippery tree-fungus travels
untroubled to my mouth.

Who's Looking?

Diggers and drills send old Peking flying
into nostrils and lungs. Tree-bark is blackened.
Picture him here in this haze that blocks the sun
among the Gucci bags and Starbucks, and the only rickshaw
a straining metal monument.

Dust from his China may be in my head, but his China
is not mine nor mine his, for this is a country
where slow rivers have been smartened up and ordered off
to service rice-fields and factories. Come down,
come down into the stink of this hutong,

come down to the bicycling grandmothers, and look –
a sweet-potato seller! Breathe the earthy steam,
get the scald of the flesh. Come and sit on a *k'ang*,
split melon seeds with your front teeth. Spit.
Belly-laugh again.

He will lift up his eyes beyond the concrete and steel
towards the little hills around Hailung –
not all of them have been carted off for cities.
He will look to where the Thousand Peaks
still point to the sky.

Traveller Talk

basically Machu Picchu ridiculous and then we did Lake Tanganyika such a disappointment just so rude we virtually had to crawl literally finally got on the M6 oh what part of Manchester my brother-in-law's aunt had the same trouble after her hip best at the airport never at the airport what rate did you get euros or dollars they don't care do they

have you tried chewing star anise health and safety gone mad that's what's wrong with the place now you must go to St Petersburg Panama Canal actually met this really interesting couple no they don't bother do they we have so much to learn from them he never tips on principle absolutely filthy you wouldn't believe full of McDonalds these days no never buy at the hotel always buy at the hotel how much do you think no go on go on guess

And why go north of Beijing? Don't go north of Beijing. Come south with us. See the Terra Cotta Army, Three Gorges and all. Don't go north. Basically nothing there. Nothing worth seeing north of Beijing. Nothing at all.

the noise of what is to come
the small silence of now

The Temple Bell

Tap, hammer and tap.
In its making, a shy energy
announces when the metal is ready.

Once hung and struck, world
spins in spirals into and beyond
human knowing. Parabolas of sound

will balloon down the bowl of the valley
and whorl in the ear of the universe
for ever.

Knocking on Manchuria's Door

You'd remember if you saw him.
Mister Corkey is an old man, his students joke
though he's only twenty-something, but it's the hair,
whitened by Beidaihe sun.

Do you know this person? Have you heard tell of him?
He's keen on sport, likes a good story,
and is very serious about God.
Oh, a while ago, seventy-something years to be true.
He knew these streets like the back of his hand.
Long time no see. *Hǎo jiǔ bú jiàn.*

Why?

Why have you come here?
Are your reasons political? Religious?
No. Only reasons of filial piety.
Ah, filial piety is good. Welcome.

Wild Gooseberries of Hailung

1

Walls sagging, roof on a terrible tilt,
rubble filling the arch of the church door
where Gao K'e Li came and went, years before he was Dad.

I hold the photo up for comparison, count bricks
between the ruined windows, a crooked one still in place
above where two solemn newly-weds posed

among lily-feet grandmas and mothers and sisters
and to the right of the picture, the men, with Gao K'e Li
who had conducted the ceremony.

I'm clambering through something like brambles.
Wild yellow gooseberries are ripening,
sweet to suck.

ll

We have found the place of the Hill of the Dead
but the dead are gone and the houses of the dead are gone
and even the grave of Deacon Wang's mother
has been quarried away for city hardcore.

We are all descendants –
the insects that jump in this spiky grass
and Deacon Wang herself, and the grass
holding us in communion.

Manners

They are saying
Your father brought us the Good News.
He was like Saint Paul.
We had a long, hard winter
and now our harvest is rich –

and they dash looks at each other, not at me.
Is *furrowed* right for their brows?
I want to unlearn *inscrutable*.

—

We are sharing a Shenyang Hotpot.
Chopsticks dip and pick like cranes' beaks,
steaming fragments are dropped into my bowl.

No room for talk in a nodding head or a munching mouth.
No protocol in warm sweet almond milk.

The Old Missionaries

1 Family

They raised the marble stones of Empire
chiselled with the names of their dead children.

The wives had God in their hearts too,
no time for sentiment, faith like a mule.

Fred's proposal came in a telegram from China.
Annie's answer, from Donegal –

'Coming'.

ll Ida Mitchell's Mandarin Teacher Speaks

Writing is beyond them. Even after long instruction,
their characters are poor. But this Little Miss
attends carefully for the four tones.
Her mistakes are done with gracious fooling.

She is a doctor, an Ireland person, *Àiĕrlán rén*.
She has cured the wife of Wang from opium sleep
by means of water and vomiting
but the widow of Lu she could not help. They say
she touched the widow's lily-feet and sang to her.

The Little Miss can pronounce, very correctly,
'I want a hospital. It is called Castle in the Air'.

lll Lost in Transubstantiation

Body and Blood.
Symbols. Reminders. Tricks?
No, we are not cannibals.
May we celebrate the Eighth Moon with you?
We shall meet again to discuss
the position of dragons.

IV Support

From the shipyard, from the ropeworks,
from the farms, the fields,
from the men, the women, their children –
pennies for the missions.

V The Women

Annie bore a brood in Manchuria and buried half of them.
Mamie spoke the best Mandarin of all the missionaries
and scared bandits off playing the organ and flute.
Dot held the fort in HsinMin,
was buried in Belfast with wild flowers.
Marion hand-delivered an important letter.

Single women, obedient or heartsick wives,
they were nurses, teachers:
Hester, Joey, Margaret, Agnes, Ruth, Lillie, May, Janie, Sara,
Alice and more ,
and doctors: Agatha, Elizabeth, Eileen, Rachel, Fedya, Emma,
Ethel, Ann, Sara the consultant surgeon,
Dorothy known as Wiggy,
and Isabel known as Ida who finally got her hospital
where she operated, instructed, died at thirty-seven.
Only grass is there now.

The Prison

Five minutes for eating.
Five minutes for lavatory.
Ten minutes for reading.
Six hours for sleeping.

Morning running.
Breaking stones, eight hours.
Méiyǒu zìyóu , no freedom.
Handcuffs.

There is no exit pass.
You go out, you are shot.
You are here
because you did or said evil things.

My father played racquet and ball games
in this underground prison in the days
when it was a gym,
the best, they said, in Manchuria.

A squash-ball
smashes,
ricochets in corners
of dank brick.

The Censor

Any mention of places, dates or massacres
and their letters would never reach home –
they all knew that,

and they had also been informed
that for any of them held as hostage
no ransom would be paid.

This will be hand-delivered,
so I can write more freely.
If I am taken, it may be a little longer

before I can see you all again.

A Little Dusting of Flour

for Denis Campbell

Your letter of October 29th arrived this morning.
I could just imagine you writing in the manse kitchen
with all your baking going on at the same time.

Back in the yeasty place of pre-naming
half a world away, he was there
in the smells and scraps of baking bread,

at his window a pink-and-grey Derry afternoon
and a soft rain, like this,
falling.

Letters Home are more Precious than Letters From Home

or so it seems, because the letters home
are handed from parent to brothers and sisters
or shared, heads touching.

They are out in Nancy's Kesh in a breast pocket,
carried across a field. They are read aloud
to wise noddings, their stories stored, to be told again.

A bold pen marks what his father has selected
to sound from his own pulpit.
Finally the letters home are folded again

and softly layered in a box on a shelf
to be dusted around and over,
touched by a finger...

and those arriving *from* home,
how quickly they are grabbed and ripped open,
how greedily devoured and re-devoured and how

lightly set aside, their job done.
He is on solid rock.
He could take on the very devil himself.

My Grandmother at Home

pressing the blotter to her bold loops, starting another page.
Then his address, its slashes and curves carefully copied,
the envelope sealed and entrusted through Maghera to Belfast
to Siberia to Manchuria.

Her news is fine wire threading his letters home:
So Uncle Fred's been ill – it's a good thing
he chased out the germs with Woodbine. When he wrote
This will be hand-delivered, so I can write more freely ...

and if I am taken, it may be a little longer
before I can see you all again,
her heart turned over. She well understood
from her own brother's quiet madness that exile

could be for ever. Freezing Ireland had appalled her at first
but she made Culnady into the place her children dreamed of
when sent to school or called far away on God's business.
She knew the meaning of home all right, my grandmother.

The girl who'd swum in Paleokastritsa, who spoke Greek first,
the woman who held no memory more sweet
than the tree-ripened figs of Patras, she it was
who'd stroke our infant heads, her guttural *Ach!*

a breath spanning a continent.

Tonghua

His bed was three chairs the time he came
to check on Tonghua's new church. The *craic* was good.
Cabbage soup for breakfast with young Pastor Bi.
He'd forgotten his camera, a pity, keen for his folks
to see the light on the river, how it curved.

We brought you a Church that is yours now, in your keeping,
said the missionaries. Now their ageing children come
for something not fathomed, felt at the fingertips, seen
through a glass darkly. Memorial characters are traced
by an untutored hand.

In Pastor Qu's high stylish house of God
I climb unfinished marble stairs to the hymn
of the carpenter hammering, hammering home
to hold and hold, and up I climb and out into bright air
in a cradle of hills.

Symposium

The one says,
Not with instruction but by example.
We bring help, medicine, and Good News.
This is our Dào.

The other says,
There is Dào – the way.
There is also Wú Wéi –
action through non-action.

Gentle forces.
The coherence of his calling
never more clear.
God or no-God,

minds are counterpoised
in harmony.
Mountain temple priest
and Tony from Derry agree:

Our hearts are the same.

Goddess of Mercy

She's a hunk of heathenry, a graven image, an idol,
not a Presbyterian or even a Christian of any sort, yet she holds
her place on the mantelpiece, minding the changes,
watching the young man who brought her home

grow old. There were days in his life when he would palm her.
He taught us how to say her name, *Guān Yīn*.
Her mild ivory gaze is on my mother, in the big chair now.
They are keeping up with the rugby, cheering Ronan O'Gara.

Surface Light

Here on Carrickfad
sea-urchins huddle in the white beds of their hollows,

anemones clot in clefts where wet barnacles tick,
pale slabs of sea hang on slate horizons.

The books in his silent study do not reveal
but hide. This, here, is my father –

a rock, solid on rock, on bladder-wrack,
blending with the lie of the land

and more clearly here, where he's framed by the big pool
that turns him round, bold against cloud.

The Elderly Children of the Missionaries

are blazing a new tourist-trail
using memoirs, letters, scraps laid down in attics
jammed in with stiff photos of forgotten faces.
But now drawers are opened, fluttery papers unfolded,
spectacles located, travel agents engaged.

The people who live on the tourist route will not say
Dà bízi which is Big-Nose,
nor will they draw undue attention
to the underground river at Benxi that ran unknown
far below the missionaries' feet all the years they were there
and all the millennia before that, and still flows
in its own icy fluorescence with newly-installed dragons.
Maintaining the Confucian convention of politeness,
the people will say, "Welcome. When we were poor and sick,
your grandfather, your great-aunt, your father
came to us, brought us the Good News, like Saint Paul,"

and they will walk with the tourists through long grass
to a place where History waits to greet them with empty hands.
When the visitors, shifting their feet among jumping insects,
ask, "Could it be that our parents or grandparents
walked and talked with your own, in this very spot?"
they will answer, "It is possible" – nothing more,
because the past is dark and far
from definite. But the elderly children
will find their missionary ancestors
everywhere.

The Lake

I am remembering the Lake at Hou Hai,
its white ornamental bridges,

willows weeping to its edges
and the lilies lifting skyward

and I remember that when winter came
a slow moon shifted through cloud over the frosted willows

and below the ice, the flowers crowding
to lay down their story.

Indigo Dreams Publishing Ltd
24, Forest Houses
Cookworthy Moor
Halwill
Beaworthy
Devon
EX21 5UU
www.indigodreams.co.uk